# Monthly Budget planner

BILL ORGANIZER AND
EXPENSES TRACKER

| MONTH: | YEAR: |
|---|---|

## INCOME

| | |
|---|---|
| | |
| | |
| | |
| | |
| TOTAL: | |

## OUTCOME

| | |
|---|---|
| | |
| | |
| | |
| | |
| TOTAL: | |

## EXPENDITURE

| BILLS | AMOUNT | DATE | PAID |
|---|---|---|---|
| | | | |
| | | | |
| | | | |
| | | | |
| | | | |
| | | | |
| | | | |
| | | | |

## CATEGORY

| Utilities | | | | |
|---|---|---|---|---|
| | | | | |
| | | | | |
| | | | | |
| | | | | |
| | | | | |
| | | | | |
| | | | | |

# WEEKLY

| MON | TUE | WED | THU | FRI | SAT | SUN |
|-----|-----|-----|-----|-----|-----|-----|
|     |     |     |     |     |     |     |

# CATEGORY

# EXPENDITURE

| BILLS | AMOUNT | DATE | PAID |
|---|---|---|---|
| | | | |
| | | | |
| | | | |
| | | | |
| | | | |
| | | | |
| | | | |
| | | | |
| | | | |
| | | | |
| | | | |
| | | | |
| | | | |
| | | | |

# CATEGORY

# CATEGORY

# SAVING PLAN

| DATE | DESCRIPTION | SAVING FOR | AMOUNT |
|------|-------------|------------|--------|
|      |             |            |        |
|      |             |            |        |
|      |             |            |        |
|      |             |            |        |
|      |             |            |        |
|      |             |            |        |
|      |             |            |        |
|      |             |            |        |
|      |             |            |        |
|      |             |            |        |
|      |             |            |        |
|      |             |            |        |
|      |             |            |        |
|      |             |            |        |
|      |             |            |        |
|      |             |            |        |
|      |             |            |        |
|      |             |   TOTAL:   |        |

# SAVING PLAN

| DATE | DESCRIPTION | SAVING FOR | AMOUNT |
|------|-------------|------------|--------|
|      |             |            |        |
|      |             |            |        |
|      |             |            |        |
|      |             |            |        |
|      |             |            |        |
|      |             |            |        |
|      |             |            |        |
|      |             |            |        |
|      |             |            |        |
|      |             |            |        |
|      |             |            |        |
|      |             |            |        |
|      |             |            |        |
|      |             |            |        |
|      |             |            |        |
|      |             |            |        |
|      |             |   TOTAL:   |        |

| MONTH: | YEAR: |
|---|---|

## INCOME

|  |  |
|---|---|
|  |  |
|  |  |
|  |  |
|  |  |
| TOTAL: |  |

## OUTCOME

|  |  |
|---|---|
|  |  |
|  |  |
|  |  |
|  |  |
| TOTAL: |  |

## EXPENDITURE

| BILLS | AMOUNT | DATE | PAID |
|---|---|---|---|
|  |  |  |  |
|  |  |  |  |
|  |  |  |  |
|  |  |  |  |
|  |  |  |  |
|  |  |  |  |
|  |  |  |  |
|  |  |  |  |

## CATEGORY

| Utilities |  |  |  |  |
|---|---|---|---|---|
|  |  |  |  |  |
|  |  |  |  |  |
|  |  |  |  |  |
|  |  |  |  |  |
|  |  |  |  |  |
|  |  |  |  |  |
|  |  |  |  |  |
|  |  |  |  |  |

# WEEKLY

| MON | TUE | WED | THU | FRI | SAT | SUN |
|-----|-----|-----|-----|-----|-----|-----|
|     |     |     |     |     |     |     |

# CATEGORY

# EXPENDITURE

| BILLS | AMOUNT | DATE | PAID |
|-------|--------|------|------|
|       |        |      |      |
|       |        |      |      |
|       |        |      |      |
|       |        |      |      |
|       |        |      |      |
|       |        |      |      |
|       |        |      |      |
|       |        |      |      |
|       |        |      |      |
|       |        |      |      |
|       |        |      |      |
|       |        |      |      |
|       |        |      |      |
|       |        |      |      |
|       |        |      |      |

# CATEGORY

|   |   |   |   |   |   |
|---|---|---|---|---|---|
|   |   |   |   |   |   |
|   |   |   |   |   |   |
|   |   |   |   |   |   |
|   |   |   |   |   |   |
|   |   |   |   |   |   |
|   |   |   |   |   |   |
|   |   |   |   |   |   |
|   |   |   |   |   |   |
|   |   |   |   |   |   |
|   |   |   |   |   |   |
|   |   |   |   |   |   |
|   |   |   |   |   |   |
|   |   |   |   |   |   |
|   |   |   |   |   |   |
|   |   |   |   |   |   |

CATEGORY

# SAVING PLAN

| DATE | DESCRIPTION | SAVING FOR | AMOUNT |
|---|---|---|---|
| | | | |
| | | | |
| | | | |
| | | | |
| | | | |
| | | | |
| | | | |
| | | | |
| | | | |
| | | | |
| | | | |
| | | | |
| | | | |
| | | | |
| | | | |
| | | | |
| | | TOTAL: | |

# SAVING PLAN

| DATE | DESCRIPTION | SAVING FOR | AMOUNT |
|------|-------------|------------|--------|
|      |             |            |        |
|      |             |            |        |
|      |             |            |        |
|      |             |            |        |
|      |             |            |        |
|      |             |            |        |
|      |             |            |        |
|      |             |            |        |
|      |             |            |        |
|      |             |            |        |
|      |             |            |        |
|      |             |            |        |
|      |             |            |        |
|      |             |            |        |
|      |             |            |        |
|      |             |            |        |
|      |             |    TOTAL:  |        |

MONTH: YEAR:

## INCOME

|  |  |
|---|---|
|  |  |
|  |  |
|  |  |
|  |  |
| TOTAL: |  |

## OUTCOME

|  |  |
|---|---|
|  |  |
|  |  |
|  |  |
|  |  |
| TOTAL: |  |

## EXPENDITURE

| BILLS | AMOUNT | DATE | PAID |
|---|---|---|---|
|  |  |  |  |
|  |  |  |  |
|  |  |  |  |
|  |  |  |  |
|  |  |  |  |
|  |  |  |  |
|  |  |  |  |

## CATEGORY

| Utilities |  |  |  |  |
|---|---|---|---|---|
|  |  |  |  |  |
|  |  |  |  |  |
|  |  |  |  |  |
|  |  |  |  |  |
|  |  |  |  |  |
|  |  |  |  |  |
|  |  |  |  |  |

# WEEKLY

| MON | TUE | WED | THU | FRI | SAT | SUN |
|-----|-----|-----|-----|-----|-----|-----|
|     |     |     |     |     |     |     |

# CATEGORY

## EXPENDITURE

| BILLS | AMOUNT | DATE | PAID |
|-------|--------|------|------|
|       |        |      |      |
|       |        |      |      |
|       |        |      |      |
|       |        |      |      |
|       |        |      |      |
|       |        |      |      |
|       |        |      |      |
|       |        |      |      |
|       |        |      |      |
|       |        |      |      |
|       |        |      |      |
|       |        |      |      |
|       |        |      |      |
|       |        |      |      |

## CATEGORY

|   |   |   |   |   |   |
|---|---|---|---|---|---|
|   |   |   |   |   |   |
|   |   |   |   |   |   |
|   |   |   |   |   |   |
|   |   |   |   |   |   |
|   |   |   |   |   |   |
|   |   |   |   |   |   |
|   |   |   |   |   |   |
|   |   |   |   |   |   |
|   |   |   |   |   |   |
|   |   |   |   |   |   |
|   |   |   |   |   |   |
|   |   |   |   |   |   |
|   |   |   |   |   |   |
|   |   |   |   |   |   |

# CATEGORY

# SAVING PLAN

| DATE | DESCRIPTION | SAVING FOR | AMOUNT |
|------|-------------|------------|--------|
|      |             |            |        |
|      |             |            |        |
|      |             |            |        |
|      |             |            |        |
|      |             |            |        |
|      |             |            |        |
|      |             |            |        |
|      |             |            |        |
|      |             |            |        |
|      |             |            |        |
|      |             |            |        |
|      |             |            |        |
|      |             |            |        |
|      |             |            |        |
|      |             |            |        |
|      |             |            |        |
|      |             |            |        |
|      |             | TOTAL:     |        |

# SAVING PLAN

| DATE | DESCRIPTION | SAVING FOR | AMOUNT |
|------|-------------|------------|--------|
|      |             |            |        |
|      |             |            |        |
|      |             |            |        |
|      |             |            |        |
|      |             |            |        |
|      |             |            |        |
|      |             |            |        |
|      |             |            |        |
|      |             |            |        |
|      |             |            |        |
|      |             |            |        |
|      |             |            |        |
|      |             |            |        |
|      |             |            |        |
|      |             |            |        |
|      |             |            |        |
|      |             |    TOTAL:  |        |

| MONTH: | YEAR: |
|---|---|

## INCOME

|  |  |
|---|---|
|  |  |
|  |  |
|  |  |
|  |  |
| TOTAL: |  |

## OUTCOME

|  |  |
|---|---|
|  |  |
|  |  |
|  |  |
|  |  |
| TOTAL: |  |

## EXPENDITURE

| BILLS | AMOUNT | DATE | PAID |
|---|---|---|---|
|  |  |  |  |
|  |  |  |  |
|  |  |  |  |
|  |  |  |  |
|  |  |  |  |
|  |  |  |  |
|  |  |  |  |
|  |  |  |  |

## CATEGORY

| Utilities |  |  |  |  |
|---|---|---|---|---|
|  |  |  |  |  |
|  |  |  |  |  |
|  |  |  |  |  |
|  |  |  |  |  |
|  |  |  |  |  |
|  |  |  |  |  |
|  |  |  |  |  |
|  |  |  |  |  |

# WEEKLY

| MON | TUE | WED | THU | FRI | SAT | SUN |
|-----|-----|-----|-----|-----|-----|-----|
|     |     |     |     |     |     |     |

# CATEGORY

## EXPENDITURE

| BILLS | AMOUNT | DATE | PAID |
|-------|--------|------|------|
|       |        |      |      |
|       |        |      |      |
|       |        |      |      |
|       |        |      |      |
|       |        |      |      |
|       |        |      |      |
|       |        |      |      |
|       |        |      |      |
|       |        |      |      |
|       |        |      |      |
|       |        |      |      |
|       |        |      |      |
|       |        |      |      |
|       |        |      |      |

## CATEGORY

|   |   |   |   |   |   |
|---|---|---|---|---|---|
|   |   |   |   |   |   |
|   |   |   |   |   |   |
|   |   |   |   |   |   |
|   |   |   |   |   |   |
|   |   |   |   |   |   |
|   |   |   |   |   |   |
|   |   |   |   |   |   |
|   |   |   |   |   |   |
|   |   |   |   |   |   |
|   |   |   |   |   |   |
|   |   |   |   |   |   |
|   |   |   |   |   |   |
|   |   |   |   |   |   |
|   |   |   |   |   |   |

# CATEGORY

# SAVING PLAN

| DATE | DESCRIPTION | SAVING FOR | AMOUNT |
|------|-------------|------------|--------|
|      |             |            |        |
|      |             |            |        |
|      |             |            |        |
|      |             |            |        |
|      |             |            |        |
|      |             |            |        |
|      |             |            |        |
|      |             |            |        |
|      |             |            |        |
|      |             |            |        |
|      |             |            |        |
|      |             |            |        |
|      |             |            |        |
|      |             |            |        |
|      |             |            |        |
|      |             |            |        |
|      |             |     TOTAL: |        |

# SAVING PLAN

| DATE | DESCRIPTION | SAVING FOR | AMOUNT |
|------|-------------|------------|--------|
|      |             |            |        |
|      |             |            |        |
|      |             |            |        |
|      |             |            |        |
|      |             |            |        |
|      |             |            |        |
|      |             |            |        |
|      |             |            |        |
|      |             |            |        |
|      |             |            |        |
|      |             |            |        |
|      |             |            |        |
|      |             |            |        |
|      |             |            |        |
|      |             |            |        |
|      |             |            |        |
|      |             |   TOTAL:   |        |

MONTH: YEAR:

| INCOME | | | OUTCOME | |
|---|---|---|---|---|
| | | | | |
| | | | | |
| | | | | |
| | | | | |
| TOTAL: | | | TOTAL: | |

## EXPENDITURE

| BILLS | AMOUNT | DATE | PAID |
|---|---|---|---|
| | | | |
| | | | |
| | | | |
| | | | |
| | | | |
| | | | |
| | | | |
| | | | |

## CATEGORY

| Utilities | | | | |
|---|---|---|---|---|
| | | | | |
| | | | | |
| | | | | |
| | | | | |
| | | | | |
| | | | | |
| | | | | |
| | | | | |

# WEEKLY

| MON | TUE | WED | THU | FRI | SAT | SUN |
|-----|-----|-----|-----|-----|-----|-----|
|     |     |     |     |     |     |     |

# CATEGORY

# EXPENDITURE

| BILLS | AMOUNT | DATE | PAID |
|-------|--------|------|------|
|       |        |      |      |
|       |        |      |      |
|       |        |      |      |
|       |        |      |      |
|       |        |      |      |
|       |        |      |      |
|       |        |      |      |
|       |        |      |      |
|       |        |      |      |
|       |        |      |      |
|       |        |      |      |
|       |        |      |      |
|       |        |      |      |
|       |        |      |      |

# CATEGORY

|   |   |   |   |   |   |
|---|---|---|---|---|---|
|   |   |   |   |   |   |
|   |   |   |   |   |   |
|   |   |   |   |   |   |
|   |   |   |   |   |   |
|   |   |   |   |   |   |
|   |   |   |   |   |   |
|   |   |   |   |   |   |
|   |   |   |   |   |   |
|   |   |   |   |   |   |
|   |   |   |   |   |   |
|   |   |   |   |   |   |
|   |   |   |   |   |   |
|   |   |   |   |   |   |
|   |   |   |   |   |   |

CATEGORY

# SAVING PLAN

| DATE | DESCRIPTION | SAVING FOR | AMOUNT |
|------|-------------|------------|--------|
|      |             |            |        |
|      |             |            |        |
|      |             |            |        |
|      |             |            |        |
|      |             |            |        |
|      |             |            |        |
|      |             |            |        |
|      |             |            |        |
|      |             |            |        |
|      |             |            |        |
|      |             |            |        |
|      |             |            |        |
|      |             |            |        |
|      |             |            |        |
|      |             |            |        |
|      |             |            |        |
|      |             | TOTAL:     |        |

# SAVING PLAN

| DATE | DESCRIPTION | SAVING FOR | AMOUNT |
|------|-------------|------------|--------|
|      |             |            |        |
|      |             |            |        |
|      |             |            |        |
|      |             |            |        |
|      |             |            |        |
|      |             |            |        |
|      |             |            |        |
|      |             |            |        |
|      |             |            |        |
|      |             |            |        |
|      |             |            |        |
|      |             |            |        |
|      |             |            |        |
|      |             |            |        |
|      |             |            |        |
|      |             |            |        |
|      |             |            |        |
|      |             |   TOTAL:   |        |

MONTH:                              YEAR:

| INCOME | |
|---|---|
|  |  |
|  |  |
|  |  |
|  |  |
| TOTAL: |  |

| OUTCOME | |
|---|---|
|  |  |
|  |  |
|  |  |
|  |  |
| TOTAL: |  |

## EXPENDITURE

| BILLS | AMOUNT | DATE | PAID |
|---|---|---|---|
|  |  |  |  |
|  |  |  |  |
|  |  |  |  |
|  |  |  |  |
|  |  |  |  |
|  |  |  |  |
|  |  |  |  |
|  |  |  |  |

## CATEGORY

| Utilities | | | | | |
|---|---|---|---|---|---|
|  |  |  |  |  |  |
|  |  |  |  |  |  |
|  |  |  |  |  |  |
|  |  |  |  |  |  |
|  |  |  |  |  |  |
|  |  |  |  |  |  |
|  |  |  |  |  |  |
|  |  |  |  |  |  |

# WEEKLY

| MON | TUE | WED | THU | FRI | SAT | SUN |
|-----|-----|-----|-----|-----|-----|-----|
|     |     |     |     |     |     |     |

# CATEGORY

# EXPENDITURE

| BILLS | AMOUNT | DATE | PAID |
|-------|--------|------|------|
|       |        |      |      |
|       |        |      |      |
|       |        |      |      |
|       |        |      |      |
|       |        |      |      |
|       |        |      |      |
|       |        |      |      |
|       |        |      |      |
|       |        |      |      |
|       |        |      |      |
|       |        |      |      |
|       |        |      |      |
|       |        |      |      |
|       |        |      |      |
|       |        |      |      |
|       |        |      |      |

# CATEGORY

|   |   |   |   |   |   |
|---|---|---|---|---|---|
|   |   |   |   |   |   |
|   |   |   |   |   |   |
|   |   |   |   |   |   |
|   |   |   |   |   |   |
|   |   |   |   |   |   |
|   |   |   |   |   |   |
|   |   |   |   |   |   |
|   |   |   |   |   |   |
|   |   |   |   |   |   |
|   |   |   |   |   |   |
|   |   |   |   |   |   |
|   |   |   |   |   |   |
|   |   |   |   |   |   |
|   |   |   |   |   |   |
|   |   |   |   |   |   |
|   |   |   |   |   |   |

# CATEGORY

# SAVING PLAN

| DATE | DESCRIPTION | SAVING FOR | AMOUNT |
|------|-------------|------------|--------|
|      |             |            |        |
|      |             |            |        |
|      |             |            |        |
|      |             |            |        |
|      |             |            |        |
|      |             |            |        |
|      |             |            |        |
|      |             |            |        |
|      |             |            |        |
|      |             |            |        |
|      |             |            |        |
|      |             |            |        |
|      |             |            |        |
|      |             |            |        |
|      |             |            |        |
|      |             |            |        |
|      |             |     TOTAL: |        |

# SAVING PLAN

| DATE | DESCRIPTION | SAVING FOR | AMOUNT |
|------|-------------|------------|--------|
|      |             |            |        |
|      |             |            |        |
|      |             |            |        |
|      |             |            |        |
|      |             |            |        |
|      |             |            |        |
|      |             |            |        |
|      |             |            |        |
|      |             |            |        |
|      |             |            |        |
|      |             |            |        |
|      |             |            |        |
|      |             |            |        |
|      |             |            |        |
|      |             |            |        |
|      |             |            |        |
|      |             |     TOTAL: |        |

| MONTH: | YEAR: |
|---|---|

## INCOME

|   |   |
|---|---|
|   |   |
|   |   |
|   |   |
|   |   |
| TOTAL: |   |

## OUTCOME

|   |   |
|---|---|
|   |   |
|   |   |
|   |   |
|   |   |
| TOTAL: |   |

## EXPENDITURE

| BILLS | AMOUNT | DATE | PAID |
|---|---|---|---|
|   |   |   |   |
|   |   |   |   |
|   |   |   |   |
|   |   |   |   |
|   |   |   |   |
|   |   |   |   |
|   |   |   |   |

## CATEGORY

| Utilities |   |   |   |   |   |
|---|---|---|---|---|---|
|   |   |   |   |   |   |
|   |   |   |   |   |   |
|   |   |   |   |   |   |
|   |   |   |   |   |   |
|   |   |   |   |   |   |
|   |   |   |   |   |   |
|   |   |   |   |   |   |

# WEEKLY

| MON | TUE | WED | THU | FRI | SAT | SUN |
|-----|-----|-----|-----|-----|-----|-----|
|     |     |     |     |     |     |     |

# CATEGORY

# EXPENDITURE

| BILLS | AMOUNT | DATE | PAID |
|-------|--------|------|------|
|       |        |      |      |
|       |        |      |      |
|       |        |      |      |
|       |        |      |      |
|       |        |      |      |
|       |        |      |      |
|       |        |      |      |
|       |        |      |      |
|       |        |      |      |
|       |        |      |      |
|       |        |      |      |
|       |        |      |      |
|       |        |      |      |
|       |        |      |      |

# CATEGORY

# CATEGORY

# SAVING PLAN

| DATE | DESCRIPTION | SAVING FOR | AMOUNT |
|------|-------------|------------|--------|
|      |             |            |        |
|      |             |            |        |
|      |             |            |        |
|      |             |            |        |
|      |             |            |        |
|      |             |            |        |
|      |             |            |        |
|      |             |            |        |
|      |             |            |        |
|      |             |            |        |
|      |             |            |        |
|      |             |            |        |
|      |             |            |        |
|      |             |            |        |
|      |             |            |        |
|      |             |            |        |
|      |             |            |        |
|      |             |            |        |
|      |             | TOTAL:     |        |

# SAVING PLAN

| DATE | DESCRIPTION | SAVING FOR | AMOUNT |
|------|-------------|------------|--------|
|      |             |            |        |
|      |             |            |        |
|      |             |            |        |
|      |             |            |        |
|      |             |            |        |
|      |             |            |        |
|      |             |            |        |
|      |             |            |        |
|      |             |            |        |
|      |             |            |        |
|      |             |            |        |
|      |             |            |        |
|      |             |            |        |
|      |             |            |        |
|      |             |            |        |
|      |             |            |        |
|      |             |     TOTAL: |        |

MONTH:                              YEAR:

| INCOME | |
|---|---|
|  |  |
|  |  |
|  |  |
|  |  |
| TOTAL: |  |

| OUTCOME | |
|---|---|
|  |  |
|  |  |
|  |  |
|  |  |
| TOTAL: |  |

## EXPENDITURE

| BILLS | AMOUNT | DATE | PAID |
|---|---|---|---|
|  |  |  |  |
|  |  |  |  |
|  |  |  |  |
|  |  |  |  |
|  |  |  |  |
|  |  |  |  |
|  |  |  |  |
|  |  |  |  |

## CATEGORY

| Utilities | | | | | |
|---|---|---|---|---|---|
|  |  |  |  |  |  |
|  |  |  |  |  |  |
|  |  |  |  |  |  |
|  |  |  |  |  |  |
|  |  |  |  |  |  |
|  |  |  |  |  |  |
|  |  |  |  |  |  |
|  |  |  |  |  |  |

# WEEKLY

| MON | TUE | WED | THU | FRI | SAT | SUN |
|-----|-----|-----|-----|-----|-----|-----|
|     |     |     |     |     |     |     |

# CATEGORY

| EXPENDITURE | | | |
|---|---|---|---|
| BILLS | AMOUNT | DATE | PAID |
| | | | |
| | | | |
| | | | |
| | | | |
| | | | |
| | | | |
| | | | |
| | | | |
| | | | |
| | | | |
| | | | |
| | | | |
| | | | |
| | | | |
| | | | |

| CATEGORY | | | | | |
|---|---|---|---|---|---|
| | | | | | |
| | | | | | |
| | | | | | |
| | | | | | |
| | | | | | |
| | | | | | |
| | | | | | |
| | | | | | |
| | | | | | |
| | | | | | |
| | | | | | |
| | | | | | |
| | | | | | |
| | | | | | |
| | | | | | |

CATEGORY

# SAVING PLAN

| DATE | DESCRIPTION | SAVING FOR | AMOUNT |
|------|-------------|------------|--------|
|      |             |            |        |
|      |             |            |        |
|      |             |            |        |
|      |             |            |        |
|      |             |            |        |
|      |             |            |        |
|      |             |            |        |
|      |             |            |        |
|      |             |            |        |
|      |             |            |        |
|      |             |            |        |
|      |             |            |        |
|      |             |            |        |
|      |             |            |        |
|      |             |            |        |
|      |             |            |        |
|      |             |            |        |
|      |             | TOTAL:     |        |

# SAVING PLAN

| DATE | DESCRIPTION | SAVING FOR | AMOUNT |
|------|-------------|------------|--------|
|      |             |            |        |
|      |             |            |        |
|      |             |            |        |
|      |             |            |        |
|      |             |            |        |
|      |             |            |        |
|      |             |            |        |
|      |             |            |        |
|      |             |            |        |
|      |             |            |        |
|      |             |            |        |
|      |             |            |        |
|      |             |            |        |
|      |             |            |        |
|      |             |            |        |
|      |             |            |        |
|      |             | TOTAL:     |        |

MONTH: YEAR:

## INCOME

| | |
|---|---|
| | |
| | |
| | |
| | |
| TOTAL: | |

## OUTCOME

| | |
|---|---|
| | |
| | |
| | |
| | |
| TOTAL: | |

## EXPENDITURE

| BILLS | AMOUNT | DATE | PAID |
|---|---|---|---|
| | | | |
| | | | |
| | | | |
| | | | |
| | | | |
| | | | |
| | | | |
| | | | |

## CATEGORY

| Utilities | | | | |
|---|---|---|---|---|
| | | | | |
| | | | | |
| | | | | |
| | | | | |
| | | | | |
| | | | | |
| | | | | |
| | | | | |

# WEEKLY

| MON | TUE | WED | THU | FRI | SAT | SUN |
|-----|-----|-----|-----|-----|-----|-----|
|     |     |     |     |     |     |     |

# CATEGORY

## EXPENDITURE

| BILLS | AMOUNT | DATE | PAID |
|---|---|---|---|
|  |  |  |  |
|  |  |  |  |
|  |  |  |  |
|  |  |  |  |
|  |  |  |  |
|  |  |  |  |
|  |  |  |  |
|  |  |  |  |
|  |  |  |  |
|  |  |  |  |
|  |  |  |  |
|  |  |  |  |
|  |  |  |  |
|  |  |  |  |

## CATEGORY

|  |  |  |  |  |  |
|---|---|---|---|---|---|
|  |  |  |  |  |  |
|  |  |  |  |  |  |
|  |  |  |  |  |  |
|  |  |  |  |  |  |
|  |  |  |  |  |  |
|  |  |  |  |  |  |
|  |  |  |  |  |  |
|  |  |  |  |  |  |
|  |  |  |  |  |  |
|  |  |  |  |  |  |
|  |  |  |  |  |  |
|  |  |  |  |  |  |
|  |  |  |  |  |  |
|  |  |  |  |  |  |

# CATEGORY

# SAVING PLAN

| DATE | DESCRIPTION | SAVING FOR | AMOUNT |
|---|---|---|---|
| | | | |
| | | | |
| | | | |
| | | | |
| | | | |
| | | | |
| | | | |
| | | | |
| | | | |
| | | | |
| | | | |
| | | | |
| | | | |
| | | | |
| | | | |
| | | | |
| | | TOTAL: | |

# SAVING PLAN

| DATE | DESCRIPTION | SAVING FOR | AMOUNT |
|------|-------------|------------|--------|
|      |             |            |        |
|      |             |            |        |
|      |             |            |        |
|      |             |            |        |
|      |             |            |        |
|      |             |            |        |
|      |             |            |        |
|      |             |            |        |
|      |             |            |        |
|      |             |            |        |
|      |             |            |        |
|      |             |            |        |
|      |             |            |        |
|      |             |            |        |
|      |             |            |        |
|      |             |            |        |
|      |             |    TOTAL:  |        |

MONTH: YEAR:

| INCOME | | | OUTCOME | |
|---|---|---|---|---|
| | | | | |
| | | | | |
| | | | | |
| | | | | |
| TOTAL: | | | TOTAL: | |

## EXPENDITURE

| BILLS | AMOUNT | DATE | PAID |
|---|---|---|---|
| | | | |
| | | | |
| | | | |
| | | | |
| | | | |
| | | | |
| | | | |
| | | | |

## CATEGORY

| Utilities | | | | |
|---|---|---|---|---|
| | | | | |
| | | | | |
| | | | | |
| | | | | |
| | | | | |
| | | | | |
| | | | | |
| | | | | |

# WEEKLY

| MON | TUE | WED | THU | FRI | SAT | SUN |
|-----|-----|-----|-----|-----|-----|-----|
|     |     |     |     |     |     |     |

# CATEGORY

## EXPENDITURE

| BILLS | AMOUNT | DATE | PAID |
|-------|--------|------|------|
|       |        |      |      |
|       |        |      |      |
|       |        |      |      |
|       |        |      |      |
|       |        |      |      |
|       |        |      |      |
|       |        |      |      |
|       |        |      |      |
|       |        |      |      |
|       |        |      |      |
|       |        |      |      |
|       |        |      |      |
|       |        |      |      |
|       |        |      |      |
|       |        |      |      |

## CATEGORY

|   |   |   |   |   |   |
|---|---|---|---|---|---|
|   |   |   |   |   |   |
|   |   |   |   |   |   |
|   |   |   |   |   |   |
|   |   |   |   |   |   |
|   |   |   |   |   |   |
|   |   |   |   |   |   |
|   |   |   |   |   |   |
|   |   |   |   |   |   |
|   |   |   |   |   |   |
|   |   |   |   |   |   |
|   |   |   |   |   |   |
|   |   |   |   |   |   |
|   |   |   |   |   |   |
|   |   |   |   |   |   |
|   |   |   |   |   |   |

# CATEGORY

# SAVING PLAN

| DATE | DESCRIPTION | SAVING FOR | AMOUNT |
|------|-------------|------------|--------|
|      |             |            |        |
|      |             |            |        |
|      |             |            |        |
|      |             |            |        |
|      |             |            |        |
|      |             |            |        |
|      |             |            |        |
|      |             |            |        |
|      |             |            |        |
|      |             |            |        |
|      |             |            |        |
|      |             |            |        |
|      |             |            |        |
|      |             |            |        |
|      |             |            |        |
|      |             |            |        |
|      |             |            |        |
|      |             |    TOTAL:  |        |

# SAVING PLAN

| DATE | DESCRIPTION | SAVING FOR | AMOUNT |
|------|-------------|------------|--------|
|      |             |            |        |
|      |             |            |        |
|      |             |            |        |
|      |             |            |        |
|      |             |            |        |
|      |             |            |        |
|      |             |            |        |
|      |             |            |        |
|      |             |            |        |
|      |             |            |        |
|      |             |            |        |
|      |             |            |        |
|      |             |            |        |
|      |             |            |        |
|      |             |            |        |
|      |             |            |        |
|      |             | TOTAL:     |        |

MONTH: YEAR:

| INCOME | | OUTCOME | |
|---|---|---|---|
| | | | |
| | | | |
| | | | |
| | | | |
| TOTAL: | | TOTAL: | |

## EXPENDITURE

| BILLS | AMOUNT | DATE | PAID |
|---|---|---|---|
| | | | |
| | | | |
| | | | |
| | | | |
| | | | |
| | | | |
| | | | |

## CATEGORY

| Utilities | | | | |
|---|---|---|---|---|
| | | | | |
| | | | | |
| | | | | |
| | | | | |
| | | | | |
| | | | | |
| | | | | |

## WEEKLY

| MON | TUE | WED | THU | FRI | SAT | SUN |
|-----|-----|-----|-----|-----|-----|-----|
|     |     |     |     |     |     |     |

## CATEGORY

| EXPENDITURE | | | | CATEGORY | | | | | |
|---|---|---|---|---|---|---|---|---|---|
| BILLS | AMOUNT | DATE | PAID | | | | | | |
| | | | | | | | | | |
| | | | | | | | | | |
| | | | | | | | | | |
| | | | | | | | | | |
| | | | | | | | | | |
| | | | | | | | | | |
| | | | | | | | | | |
| | | | | | | | | | |
| | | | | | | | | | |
| | | | | | | | | | |
| | | | | | | | | | |
| | | | | | | | | | |
| | | | | | | | | | |
| | | | | | | | | | |

CATEGORY

# SAVING PLAN

| DATE | DESCRIPTION | SAVING FOR | AMOUNT |
|------|-------------|------------|--------|
|      |             |            |        |
|      |             |            |        |
|      |             |            |        |
|      |             |            |        |
|      |             |            |        |
|      |             |            |        |
|      |             |            |        |
|      |             |            |        |
|      |             |            |        |
|      |             |            |        |
|      |             |            |        |
|      |             |            |        |
|      |             |            |        |
|      |             |            |        |
|      |             |            |        |
|      |             |            |        |
|      |             |            |        |
|      |             | TOTAL:     |        |

# SAVING PLAN

| DATE | DESCRIPTION | SAVING FOR | AMOUNT |
|------|-------------|------------|--------|
|      |             |            |        |
|      |             |            |        |
|      |             |            |        |
|      |             |            |        |
|      |             |            |        |
|      |             |            |        |
|      |             |            |        |
|      |             |            |        |
|      |             |            |        |
|      |             |            |        |
|      |             |            |        |
|      |             |            |        |
|      |             |            |        |
|      |             |            |        |
|      |             |            |        |
|      |             |    TOTAL:  |        |

MONTH:    YEAR:

## INCOME

| | |
|---|---|
| | |
| | |
| | |
| | |
| TOTAL: | |

## OUTCOME

| | |
|---|---|
| | |
| | |
| | |
| | |
| TOTAL: | |

## EXPENDITURE

| BILLS | AMOUNT | DATE | PAID |
|---|---|---|---|
| | | | |
| | | | |
| | | | |
| | | | |
| | | | |
| | | | |
| | | | |
| | | | |

## CATEGORY

| Utilities | | | | |
|---|---|---|---|---|
| | | | | |
| | | | | |
| | | | | |
| | | | | |
| | | | | |
| | | | | |
| | | | | |
| | | | | |

| WEEKLY |||||||
|---|---|---|---|---|---|---|
| MON | TUE | WED | THU | FRI | SAT | SUN |
|  |  |  |  |  |  |  |

## CATEGORY

| EXPENDITURE | | | |
|---|---|---|---|
| BILLS | AMOUNT | DATE | PAID |
| | | | |
| | | | |
| | | | |
| | | | |
| | | | |
| | | | |
| | | | |
| | | | |
| | | | |
| | | | |
| | | | |
| | | | |
| | | | |
| | | | |

## CATEGORY

# CATEGORY

# SAVING PLAN

| DATE | DESCRIPTION | SAVING FOR | AMOUNT |
|------|-------------|------------|--------|
|      |             |            |        |
|      |             |            |        |
|      |             |            |        |
|      |             |            |        |
|      |             |            |        |
|      |             |            |        |
|      |             |            |        |
|      |             |            |        |
|      |             |            |        |
|      |             |            |        |
|      |             |            |        |
|      |             |            |        |
|      |             |            |        |
|      |             |            |        |
|      |             |            |        |
|      |             |            |        |
|      |             |     TOTAL: |        |

# SAVING PLAN

| DATE | DESCRIPTION | SAVING FOR | AMOUNT |
|------|-------------|------------|--------|
|      |             |            |        |
|      |             |            |        |
|      |             |            |        |
|      |             |            |        |
|      |             |            |        |
|      |             |            |        |
|      |             |            |        |
|      |             |            |        |
|      |             |            |        |
|      |             |            |        |
|      |             |            |        |
|      |             |            |        |
|      |             |            |        |
|      |             |            |        |
|      |             |            |        |
|      |             |            |        |
|      |             |   TOTAL:   |        |

| MONTH: | YEAR: |
|---|---|

## INCOME

|  |  |
|---|---|
|  |  |
|  |  |
|  |  |
|  |  |
| TOTAL: |  |

## OUTCOME

|  |  |
|---|---|
|  |  |
|  |  |
|  |  |
|  |  |
| TOTAL: |  |

## EXPENDITURE

| BILLS | AMOUNT | DATE | PAID |
|---|---|---|---|
|  |  |  |  |
|  |  |  |  |
|  |  |  |  |
|  |  |  |  |
|  |  |  |  |
|  |  |  |  |
|  |  |  |  |
|  |  |  |  |

## CATEGORY

| Utilities |  |  |  |  |
|---|---|---|---|---|
|  |  |  |  |  |
|  |  |  |  |  |
|  |  |  |  |  |
|  |  |  |  |  |
|  |  |  |  |  |
|  |  |  |  |  |
|  |  |  |  |  |

# WEEKLY

| MON | TUE | WED | THU | FRI | SAT | SUN |
|-----|-----|-----|-----|-----|-----|-----|
|     |     |     |     |     |     |     |

# CATEGORY

## EXPENDITURE

| BILLS | AMOUNT | DATE | PAID |
|-------|--------|------|------|
|       |        |      |      |
|       |        |      |      |
|       |        |      |      |
|       |        |      |      |
|       |        |      |      |
|       |        |      |      |
|       |        |      |      |
|       |        |      |      |
|       |        |      |      |
|       |        |      |      |
|       |        |      |      |
|       |        |      |      |
|       |        |      |      |
|       |        |      |      |

## CATEGORY

|  |  |  |  |  |  |
|--|--|--|--|--|--|
|  |  |  |  |  |  |
|  |  |  |  |  |  |
|  |  |  |  |  |  |
|  |  |  |  |  |  |
|  |  |  |  |  |  |
|  |  |  |  |  |  |
|  |  |  |  |  |  |
|  |  |  |  |  |  |
|  |  |  |  |  |  |
|  |  |  |  |  |  |
|  |  |  |  |  |  |
|  |  |  |  |  |  |
|  |  |  |  |  |  |
|  |  |  |  |  |  |

## CATEGORY

# SAVING PLAN

| DATE | DESCRIPTION | SAVING FOR | AMOUNT |
|------|-------------|------------|--------|
|      |             |            |        |
|      |             |            |        |
|      |             |            |        |
|      |             |            |        |
|      |             |            |        |
|      |             |            |        |
|      |             |            |        |
|      |             |            |        |
|      |             |            |        |
|      |             |            |        |
|      |             |            |        |
|      |             |            |        |
|      |             |            |        |
|      |             |            |        |
|      |             |            |        |
|      |             |            |        |
|      |             |            |        |
|      |             |     TOTAL: |        |

# SAVING PLAN

| DATE | DESCRIPTION | SAVING FOR | AMOUNT |
|------|-------------|------------|--------|
|      |             |            |        |
|      |             |            |        |
|      |             |            |        |
|      |             |            |        |
|      |             |            |        |
|      |             |            |        |
|      |             |            |        |
|      |             |            |        |
|      |             |            |        |
|      |             |            |        |
|      |             |            |        |
|      |             |            |        |
|      |             |            |        |
|      |             |            |        |
|      |             |            |        |
|      |             |            |        |
|      |             | TOTAL:     |        |

| MONTH: | YEAR: |
|---|---|

## INCOME

|  |  |
|---|---|
|  |  |
|  |  |
|  |  |
|  |  |
| TOTAL: |  |

## OUTCOME

|  |  |
|---|---|
|  |  |
|  |  |
|  |  |
|  |  |
| TOTAL: |  |

## EXPENDITURE

| BILLS | AMOUNT | DATE | PAID |
|---|---|---|---|
|  |  |  |  |
|  |  |  |  |
|  |  |  |  |
|  |  |  |  |
|  |  |  |  |
|  |  |  |  |
|  |  |  |  |
|  |  |  |  |

## CATEGORY

| Utilities |  |  |  |  |
|---|---|---|---|---|
|  |  |  |  |  |
|  |  |  |  |  |
|  |  |  |  |  |
|  |  |  |  |  |
|  |  |  |  |  |
|  |  |  |  |  |
|  |  |  |  |  |
|  |  |  |  |  |

# WEEKLY

| MON | TUE | WED | THU | FRI | SAT | SUN |
|---|---|---|---|---|---|---|
|  |  |  |  |  |  |  |

# CATEGORY

# EXPENDITURE

| BILLS | AMOUNT | DATE | PAID |
|-------|--------|------|------|
|       |        |      |      |
|       |        |      |      |
|       |        |      |      |
|       |        |      |      |
|       |        |      |      |
|       |        |      |      |
|       |        |      |      |
|       |        |      |      |
|       |        |      |      |
|       |        |      |      |
|       |        |      |      |
|       |        |      |      |
|       |        |      |      |
|       |        |      |      |

# CATEGORY

# CATEGORY

# SAVING PLAN

| DATE | DESCRIPTION | SAVING FOR | AMOUNT |
|------|-------------|------------|--------|
|      |             |            |        |
|      |             |            |        |
|      |             |            |        |
|      |             |            |        |
|      |             |            |        |
|      |             |            |        |
|      |             |            |        |
|      |             |            |        |
|      |             |            |        |
|      |             |            |        |
|      |             |            |        |
|      |             |            |        |
|      |             |            |        |
|      |             |            |        |
|      |             |            |        |
|      |             |            |        |
|      |             |    TOTAL:  |        |

# SAVING PLAN

| DATE | DESCRIPTION | SAVING FOR | AMOUNT |
|------|-------------|------------|--------|
|      |             |            |        |
|      |             |            |        |
|      |             |            |        |
|      |             |            |        |
|      |             |            |        |
|      |             |            |        |
|      |             |            |        |
|      |             |            |        |
|      |             |            |        |
|      |             |            |        |
|      |             |            |        |
|      |             |            |        |
|      |             |            |        |
|      |             |            |        |
|      |             |            |        |
|      |             |            |        |
|      |             | TOTAL:     |        |

| MONTH: | YEAR: |
|---|---|

## INCOME

| | |
|---|---|
| | |
| | |
| | |
| | |
| TOTAL: | |

## OUTCOME

| | |
|---|---|
| | |
| | |
| | |
| | |
| TOTAL: | |

## EXPENDITURE

| BILLS | AMOUNT | DATE | PAID |
|---|---|---|---|
| | | | |
| | | | |
| | | | |
| | | | |
| | | | |
| | | | |
| | | | |
| | | | |

## CATEGORY

| Utilities | | | | | |
|---|---|---|---|---|---|
| | | | | | |
| | | | | | |
| | | | | | |
| | | | | | |
| | | | | | |
| | | | | | |
| | | | | | |

# WEEKLY

| MON | TUE | WED | THU | FRI | SAT | SUN |
|-----|-----|-----|-----|-----|-----|-----|
|     |     |     |     |     |     |     |

# CATEGORY

| EXPENDITURE | | | |
|---|---|---|---|
| BILLS | AMOUNT | DATE | PAID |
| | | | |
| | | | |
| | | | |
| | | | |
| | | | |
| | | | |
| | | | |
| | | | |
| | | | |
| | | | |
| | | | |
| | | | |
| | | | |
| | | | |

## CATEGORY

# CATEGORY

# SAVING PLAN

| DATE | DESCRIPTION | SAVING FOR | AMOUNT |
|------|-------------|------------|--------|
|      |             |            |        |
|      |             |            |        |
|      |             |            |        |
|      |             |            |        |
|      |             |            |        |
|      |             |            |        |
|      |             |            |        |
|      |             |            |        |
|      |             |            |        |
|      |             |            |        |
|      |             |            |        |
|      |             |            |        |
|      |             |            |        |
|      |             |            |        |
|      |             |            |        |
|      |             |            |        |
|      |             |    TOTAL:  |        |

# SAVING PLAN

| DATE | DESCRIPTION | SAVING FOR | AMOUNT |
|------|-------------|------------|--------|
|      |             |            |        |
|      |             |            |        |
|      |             |            |        |
|      |             |            |        |
|      |             |            |        |
|      |             |            |        |
|      |             |            |        |
|      |             |            |        |
|      |             |            |        |
|      |             |            |        |
|      |             |            |        |
|      |             |            |        |
|      |             |            |        |
|      |             |            |        |
|      |             |            |        |
|      |             |   TOTAL:   |        |

MONTH: YEAR:

## INCOME

| | |
|---|---|
| | |
| | |
| | |
| | |
| TOTAL: | |

## OUTCOME

| | |
|---|---|
| | |
| | |
| | |
| | |
| TOTAL: | |

## EXPENDITURE

| BILLS | AMOUNT | DATE | PAID |
|---|---|---|---|
| | | | |
| | | | |
| | | | |
| | | | |
| | | | |
| | | | |
| | | | |
| | | | |

## CATEGORY

| Utilities | | | | | |
|---|---|---|---|---|---|
| | | | | | |
| | | | | | |
| | | | | | |
| | | | | | |
| | | | | | |
| | | | | | |
| | | | | | |
| | | | | | |

# WEEKLY

| MON | TUE | WED | THU | FRI | SAT | SUN |
|-----|-----|-----|-----|-----|-----|-----|
|     |     |     |     |     |     |     |

# CATEGORY

## EXPENDITURE

| BILLS | AMOUNT | DATE | PAID |
|---|---|---|---|
|  |  |  |  |
|  |  |  |  |
|  |  |  |  |
|  |  |  |  |
|  |  |  |  |
|  |  |  |  |
|  |  |  |  |
|  |  |  |  |
|  |  |  |  |
|  |  |  |  |
|  |  |  |  |
|  |  |  |  |
|  |  |  |  |
|  |  |  |  |
|  |  |  |  |

## CATEGORY

|  |  |  |  |  |  |
|---|---|---|---|---|---|
|  |  |  |  |  |  |
|  |  |  |  |  |  |
|  |  |  |  |  |  |
|  |  |  |  |  |  |
|  |  |  |  |  |  |
|  |  |  |  |  |  |
|  |  |  |  |  |  |
|  |  |  |  |  |  |
|  |  |  |  |  |  |
|  |  |  |  |  |  |
|  |  |  |  |  |  |
|  |  |  |  |  |  |
|  |  |  |  |  |  |
|  |  |  |  |  |  |
|  |  |  |  |  |  |

CATEGORY

# SAVING PLAN

| DATE | DESCRIPTION | SAVING FOR | AMOUNT |
|------|-------------|------------|--------|
|      |             |            |        |
|      |             |            |        |
|      |             |            |        |
|      |             |            |        |
|      |             |            |        |
|      |             |            |        |
|      |             |            |        |
|      |             |            |        |
|      |             |            |        |
|      |             |            |        |
|      |             |            |        |
|      |             |            |        |
|      |             |            |        |
|      |             |            |        |
|      |             |            |        |
|      |             |            |        |
|      |             |            |        |
|      |             |   TOTAL:   |        |

# SAVING PLAN

| DATE | DESCRIPTION | SAVING FOR | AMOUNT |
|------|-------------|------------|--------|
|      |             |            |        |
|      |             |            |        |
|      |             |            |        |
|      |             |            |        |
|      |             |            |        |
|      |             |            |        |
|      |             |            |        |
|      |             |            |        |
|      |             |            |        |
|      |             |            |        |
|      |             |            |        |
|      |             |            |        |
|      |             |            |        |
|      |             |            |        |
|      |             |            |        |
|      |             |            |        |
|      |             | TOTAL:     |        |

MONTH: YEAR:

## INCOME

| | |
|---|---|
| | |
| | |
| | |
| | |
| TOTAL: | |

## OUTCOME

| | |
|---|---|
| | |
| | |
| | |
| | |
| TOTAL: | |

## EXPENDITURE

| BILLS | AMOUNT | DATE | PAID |
|---|---|---|---|
| | | | |
| | | | |
| | | | |
| | | | |
| | | | |
| | | | |
| | | | |
| | | | |

## CATEGORY

| Utilities | | | | | |
|---|---|---|---|---|---|
| | | | | | |
| | | | | | |
| | | | | | |
| | | | | | |
| | | | | | |
| | | | | | |
| | | | | | |
| | | | | | |

|  | WEEKLY |  |  |  |  |  |
|---|---|---|---|---|---|---|
| MON | TUE | WED | THU | FRI | SAT | SUN |
|  |  |  |  |  |  |  |

## CATEGORY

| EXPENDITURE | | | |
|---|---|---|---|
| BILLS | AMOUNT | DATE | PAID |
| | | | |
| | | | |
| | | | |
| | | | |
| | | | |
| | | | |
| | | | |
| | | | |
| | | | |
| | | | |
| | | | |
| | | | |
| | | | |
| | | | |

## CATEGORY

# CATEGORY

# CATEGORY

# SAVING PLAN

| DATE | DESCRIPTION | SAVING FOR | AMOUNT |
|------|-------------|------------|--------|
|      |             |            |        |
|      |             |            |        |
|      |             |            |        |
|      |             |            |        |
|      |             |            |        |
|      |             |            |        |
|      |             |            |        |
|      |             |            |        |
|      |             |            |        |
|      |             |            |        |
|      |             |            |        |
|      |             |            |        |
|      |             |            |        |
|      |             |            |        |
|      |             |            |        |
|      |             |            |        |
|      |             |   TOTAL:   |        |

# SAVING PLAN

| DATE | DESCRIPTION | SAVING FOR | AMOUNT |
|------|-------------|------------|--------|
|      |             |            |        |
|      |             |            |        |
|      |             |            |        |
|      |             |            |        |
|      |             |            |        |
|      |             |            |        |
|      |             |            |        |
|      |             |            |        |
|      |             |            |        |
|      |             |            |        |
|      |             |            |        |
|      |             |            |        |
|      |             |            |        |
|      |             |            |        |
|      |             |            |        |
|      |             |            |        |
|      |             |   TOTAL:   |        |

# MONTH:  YEAR:

## INCOME

| | |
|---|---|
| | |
| | |
| | |
| | |
| TOTAL: | |

## OUTCOME

| | |
|---|---|
| | |
| | |
| | |
| | |
| TOTAL: | |

## EXPENDITURE

| BILLS | AMOUNT | DATE | PAID |
|---|---|---|---|
| | | | |
| | | | |
| | | | |
| | | | |
| | | | |
| | | | |
| | | | |
| | | | |

## CATEGORY

| Utilities | | | | |
|---|---|---|---|---|
| | | | | |
| | | | | |
| | | | | |
| | | | | |
| | | | | |
| | | | | |
| | | | | |
| | | | | |

# WEEKLY

| MON | TUE | WED | THU | FRI | SAT | SUN |
|-----|-----|-----|-----|-----|-----|-----|
|     |     |     |     |     |     |     |

# CATEGORY

# EXPENDITURE

| BILLS | AMOUNT | DATE | PAID |
|---|---|---|---|
|  |  |  |  |
|  |  |  |  |
|  |  |  |  |
|  |  |  |  |
|  |  |  |  |
|  |  |  |  |
|  |  |  |  |
|  |  |  |  |
|  |  |  |  |
|  |  |  |  |
|  |  |  |  |
|  |  |  |  |
|  |  |  |  |
|  |  |  |  |
|  |  |  |  |

# CATEGORY

|  |  |  |  |  |  |
|---|---|---|---|---|---|
|  |  |  |  |  |  |
|  |  |  |  |  |  |
|  |  |  |  |  |  |
|  |  |  |  |  |  |
|  |  |  |  |  |  |
|  |  |  |  |  |  |
|  |  |  |  |  |  |
|  |  |  |  |  |  |
|  |  |  |  |  |  |
|  |  |  |  |  |  |
|  |  |  |  |  |  |
|  |  |  |  |  |  |
|  |  |  |  |  |  |
|  |  |  |  |  |  |
|  |  |  |  |  |  |

## CATEGORY

# SAVING PLAN

| DATE | DESCRIPTION | SAVING FOR | AMOUNT |
|---|---|---|---|
| | | | |
| | | | |
| | | | |
| | | | |
| | | | |
| | | | |
| | | | |
| | | | |
| | | | |
| | | | |
| | | | |
| | | | |
| | | | |
| | | | |
| | | | |
| | | TOTAL: | |

# SAVING PLAN

| DATE | DESCRIPTION | SAVING FOR | AMOUNT |
|------|-------------|------------|--------|
|      |             |            |        |
|      |             |            |        |
|      |             |            |        |
|      |             |            |        |
|      |             |            |        |
|      |             |            |        |
|      |             |            |        |
|      |             |            |        |
|      |             |            |        |
|      |             |            |        |
|      |             |            |        |
|      |             |            |        |
|      |             |            |        |
|      |             |            |        |
|      |             |      TOTAL: |        |

MONTH: YEAR:

## INCOME

| | |
|---|---|
| | |
| | |
| | |
| | |
| TOTAL: | |

## OUTCOME

| | |
|---|---|
| | |
| | |
| | |
| | |
| TOTAL: | |

## EXPENDITURE

| BILLS | AMOUNT | DATE | PAID |
|---|---|---|---|
| | | | |
| | | | |
| | | | |
| | | | |
| | | | |
| | | | |
| | | | |
| | | | |

## CATEGORY

| Utilities | | | | | |
|---|---|---|---|---|---|
| | | | | | |
| | | | | | |
| | | | | | |
| | | | | | |
| | | | | | |
| | | | | | |
| | | | | | |

## WEEKLY

| MON | TUE | WED | THU | FRI | SAT | SUN |
|-----|-----|-----|-----|-----|-----|-----|
|     |     |     |     |     |     |     |

## CATEGORY

| EXPENDITURE | | | |
|---|---|---|---|
| BILLS | AMOUNT | DATE | PAID |
| | | | |
| | | | |
| | | | |
| | | | |
| | | | |
| | | | |
| | | | |
| | | | |
| | | | |
| | | | |
| | | | |
| | | | |
| | | | |
| | | | |
| | | | |

## CATEGORY

# CATEGORY

CATEGORY

# SAVING PLAN

| DATE | DESCRIPTION | SAVING FOR | AMOUNT |
|------|-------------|------------|--------|
|      |             |            |        |
|      |             |            |        |
|      |             |            |        |
|      |             |            |        |
|      |             |            |        |
|      |             |            |        |
|      |             |            |        |
|      |             |            |        |
|      |             |            |        |
|      |             |            |        |
|      |             |            |        |
|      |             |            |        |
|      |             |            |        |
|      |             |            |        |
|      |             |            |        |
|      |             |            |        |
|      |             |            |        |
|      |             |    TOTAL:  |        |

# SAVING PLAN

| DATE | DESCRIPTION | SAVING FOR | AMOUNT |
|------|-------------|------------|--------|
|      |             |            |        |
|      |             |            |        |
|      |             |            |        |
|      |             |            |        |
|      |             |            |        |
|      |             |            |        |
|      |             |            |        |
|      |             |            |        |
|      |             |            |        |
|      |             |            |        |
|      |             |            |        |
|      |             |            |        |
|      |             |            |        |
|      |             |            |        |
|      |             |            |        |
|      |             |            |        |
|      |             |    TOTAL:  |        |

MONTH: YEAR:

| INCOME | | OUTCOME | |
|---|---|---|---|
| | | | |
| | | | |
| | | | |
| | | | |
| TOTAL: | | TOTAL: | |

## EXPENDITURE

| BILLS | AMOUNT | DATE | PAID |
|---|---|---|---|
| | | | |
| | | | |
| | | | |
| | | | |
| | | | |
| | | | |
| | | | |

## CATEGORY

| Utilities | | | | | |
|---|---|---|---|---|---|
| | | | | | |
| | | | | | |
| | | | | | |
| | | | | | |
| | | | | | |
| | | | | | |
| | | | | | |

# WEEKLY

| MON | TUE | WED | THU | FRI | SAT | SUN |
|-----|-----|-----|-----|-----|-----|-----|
|     |     |     |     |     |     |     |

# CATEGORY

## EXPENDITURE

| BILLS | AMOUNT | DATE | PAID |
|-------|--------|------|------|
|       |        |      |      |
|       |        |      |      |
|       |        |      |      |
|       |        |      |      |
|       |        |      |      |
|       |        |      |      |
|       |        |      |      |
|       |        |      |      |
|       |        |      |      |
|       |        |      |      |
|       |        |      |      |
|       |        |      |      |
|       |        |      |      |
|       |        |      |      |

## CATEGORY

|  |  |  |  |  |  |
|--|--|--|--|--|--|
|  |  |  |  |  |  |
|  |  |  |  |  |  |
|  |  |  |  |  |  |
|  |  |  |  |  |  |
|  |  |  |  |  |  |
|  |  |  |  |  |  |
|  |  |  |  |  |  |
|  |  |  |  |  |  |
|  |  |  |  |  |  |
|  |  |  |  |  |  |
|  |  |  |  |  |  |
|  |  |  |  |  |  |
|  |  |  |  |  |  |
|  |  |  |  |  |  |

## CATEGORY

# SAVING PLAN

| DATE | DESCRIPTION | SAVING FOR | AMOUNT |
|------|-------------|------------|--------|
|      |             |            |        |
|      |             |            |        |
|      |             |            |        |
|      |             |            |        |
|      |             |            |        |
|      |             |            |        |
|      |             |            |        |
|      |             |            |        |
|      |             |            |        |
|      |             |            |        |
|      |             |            |        |
|      |             |            |        |
|      |             |            |        |
|      |             |            |        |
|      |             |            |        |
|      |             |            |        |
|      |             |            |        |
|      |             |     TOTAL: |        |

# SAVING PLAN

| DATE | DESCRIPTION | SAVING FOR | AMOUNT |
|------|-------------|------------|--------|
|      |             |            |        |
|      |             |            |        |
|      |             |            |        |
|      |             |            |        |
|      |             |            |        |
|      |             |            |        |
|      |             |            |        |
|      |             |            |        |
|      |             |            |        |
|      |             |            |        |
|      |             |            |        |
|      |             |            |        |
|      |             |            |        |
|      |             |            |        |
|      |             |            |        |
|      |             |            |        |
|      |             |    TOTAL:  |        |

MONTH:  YEAR:

## INCOME

| | |
|---|---|
| | |
| | |
| | |
| | |
| TOTAL: | |

## OUTCOME

| | |
|---|---|
| | |
| | |
| | |
| | |
| TOTAL: | |

## EXPENDITURE

| BILLS | AMOUNT | DATE | PAID |
|---|---|---|---|
| | | | |
| | | | |
| | | | |
| | | | |
| | | | |
| | | | |
| | | | |

## CATEGORY

| Utilities | | | | | |
|---|---|---|---|---|---|
| | | | | | |
| | | | | | |
| | | | | | |
| | | | | | |
| | | | | | |
| | | | | | |

## WEEKLY

| MON | TUE | WED | THU | FRI | SAT | SUN |
|-----|-----|-----|-----|-----|-----|-----|
|     |     |     |     |     |     |     |

## CATEGORY

# EXPENDITURE

| BILLS | AMOUNT | DATE | PAID |
|---|---|---|---|
| | | | |
| | | | |
| | | | |
| | | | |
| | | | |
| | | | |
| | | | |
| | | | |
| | | | |
| | | | |
| | | | |
| | | | |
| | | | |
| | | | |
| | | | |

# CATEGORY

# CATEGORY

# CATEGORY

# SAVING PLAN

| DATE | DESCRIPTION | SAVING FOR | AMOUNT |
|------|-------------|------------|--------|
|      |             |            |        |
|      |             |            |        |
|      |             |            |        |
|      |             |            |        |
|      |             |            |        |
|      |             |            |        |
|      |             |            |        |
|      |             |            |        |
|      |             |            |        |
|      |             |            |        |
|      |             |            |        |
|      |             |            |        |
|      |             |            |        |
|      |             |            |        |
|      |             |            |        |
|      |             |            |        |
|      |             |      TOTAL:|        |

# SAVING PLAN

| DATE | DESCRIPTION | SAVING FOR | AMOUNT |
|------|-------------|------------|--------|
|      |             |            |        |
|      |             |            |        |
|      |             |            |        |
|      |             |            |        |
|      |             |            |        |
|      |             |            |        |
|      |             |            |        |
|      |             |            |        |
|      |             |            |        |
|      |             |            |        |
|      |             |            |        |
|      |             |            |        |
|      |             |            |        |
|      |             |            |        |
|      |             |            |        |
|      |             |            |        |
|      |             |    TOTAL:  |        |

MONTH: YEAR:

## INCOME

| | |
|---|---|
| | |
| | |
| | |
| | |
| TOTAL: | |

## OUTCOME

| | |
|---|---|
| | |
| | |
| | |
| | |
| TOTAL: | |

## EXPENDITURE

| BILLS | AMOUNT | DATE | PAID |
|---|---|---|---|
| | | | |
| | | | |
| | | | |
| | | | |
| | | | |
| | | | |
| | | | |
| | | | |

## CATEGORY

| Utilities | | | | | |
|---|---|---|---|---|---|
| | | | | | |
| | | | | | |
| | | | | | |
| | | | | | |
| | | | | | |
| | | | | | |
| | | | | | |
| | | | | | |

# WEEKLY

| MON | TUE | WED | THU | FRI | SAT | SUN |
|-----|-----|-----|-----|-----|-----|-----|
|     |     |     |     |     |     |     |

# CATEGORY

## EXPENDITURE

| BILLS | AMOUNT | DATE | PAID |
|-------|--------|------|------|
|       |        |      |      |
|       |        |      |      |
|       |        |      |      |
|       |        |      |      |
|       |        |      |      |
|       |        |      |      |
|       |        |      |      |
|       |        |      |      |
|       |        |      |      |
|       |        |      |      |
|       |        |      |      |
|       |        |      |      |
|       |        |      |      |
|       |        |      |      |

## CATEGORY

|  |  |  |  |  |  |
|--|--|--|--|--|--|
|  |  |  |  |  |  |
|  |  |  |  |  |  |
|  |  |  |  |  |  |
|  |  |  |  |  |  |
|  |  |  |  |  |  |
|  |  |  |  |  |  |
|  |  |  |  |  |  |
|  |  |  |  |  |  |
|  |  |  |  |  |  |
|  |  |  |  |  |  |
|  |  |  |  |  |  |
|  |  |  |  |  |  |
|  |  |  |  |  |  |
|  |  |  |  |  |  |

CATEGORY

# SAVING PLAN

| DATE | DESCRIPTION | SAVING FOR | AMOUNT |
|------|-------------|------------|--------|
|      |             |            |        |
|      |             |            |        |
|      |             |            |        |
|      |             |            |        |
|      |             |            |        |
|      |             |            |        |
|      |             |            |        |
|      |             |            |        |
|      |             |            |        |
|      |             |            |        |
|      |             |            |        |
|      |             |            |        |
|      |             |            |        |
|      |             |            |        |
|      |             |            |        |
|      |             |            |        |
|      |             |   TOTAL:   |        |

# SAVING PLAN

| DATE | DESCRIPTION | SAVING FOR | AMOUNT |
|------|-------------|------------|--------|
|      |             |            |        |
|      |             |            |        |
|      |             |            |        |
|      |             |            |        |
|      |             |            |        |
|      |             |            |        |
|      |             |            |        |
|      |             |            |        |
|      |             |            |        |
|      |             |            |        |
|      |             |            |        |
|      |             |            |        |
|      |             |            |        |
|      |             |            |        |
|      |             |            |        |
|      |             |            |        |
|      |             |   TOTAL:   |        |

| MONTH: | YEAR: |
|---|---|

## INCOME

| | |
|---|---|
| | |
| | |
| | |
| | |
| TOTAL: | |

## OUTCOME

| | |
|---|---|
| | |
| | |
| | |
| | |
| TOTAL: | |

## EXPENDITURE

| BILLS | AMOUNT | DATE | PAID |
|---|---|---|---|
| | | | |
| | | | |
| | | | |
| | | | |
| | | | |
| | | | |
| | | | |
| | | | |

## CATEGORY

| Utilities | | | | |
|---|---|---|---|---|
| | | | | |
| | | | | |
| | | | | |
| | | | | |
| | | | | |
| | | | | |
| | | | | |

| MON | TUE | WED | THU | FRI | SAT | SUN |
|---|---|---|---|---|---|---|
|  |  |  |  |  |  |  |

## CATEGORY

# EXPENDITURE

| BILLS | AMOUNT | DATE | PAID |
|-------|--------|------|------|
|       |        |      |      |
|       |        |      |      |
|       |        |      |      |
|       |        |      |      |
|       |        |      |      |
|       |        |      |      |
|       |        |      |      |
|       |        |      |      |
|       |        |      |      |
|       |        |      |      |
|       |        |      |      |
|       |        |      |      |
|       |        |      |      |
|       |        |      |      |

# CATEGORY

|   |   |   |   |   |   |
|---|---|---|---|---|---|
|   |   |   |   |   |   |
|   |   |   |   |   |   |
|   |   |   |   |   |   |
|   |   |   |   |   |   |
|   |   |   |   |   |   |
|   |   |   |   |   |   |
|   |   |   |   |   |   |
|   |   |   |   |   |   |
|   |   |   |   |   |   |
|   |   |   |   |   |   |
|   |   |   |   |   |   |
|   |   |   |   |   |   |
|   |   |   |   |   |   |
|   |   |   |   |   |   |

# CATEGORY

# SAVING PLAN

| DATE | DESCRIPTION | SAVING FOR | AMOUNT |
|------|-------------|------------|--------|
|      |             |            |        |
|      |             |            |        |
|      |             |            |        |
|      |             |            |        |
|      |             |            |        |
|      |             |            |        |
|      |             |            |        |
|      |             |            |        |
|      |             |            |        |
|      |             |            |        |
|      |             |            |        |
|      |             |            |        |
|      |             |            |        |
|      |             |            |        |
|      |             |            |        |
|      |             |            |        |
|      |             |    TOTAL:  |        |

# SAVING PLAN

| DATE | DESCRIPTION | SAVING FOR | AMOUNT |
|------|-------------|------------|--------|
|      |             |            |        |
|      |             |            |        |
|      |             |            |        |
|      |             |            |        |
|      |             |            |        |
|      |             |            |        |
|      |             |            |        |
|      |             |            |        |
|      |             |            |        |
|      |             |            |        |
|      |             |            |        |
|      |             |            |        |
|      |             |            |        |
|      |             |            |        |
|      |             |            |        |
|      |             |            |        |
|      |             |    TOTAL:  |        |

MONTH:                              YEAR:

## INCOME

|   |   |
|---|---|
|   |   |
|   |   |
|   |   |
|   |   |
| TOTAL: |   |

## OUTCOME

|   |   |
|---|---|
|   |   |
|   |   |
|   |   |
|   |   |
| TOTAL: |   |

## EXPENDITURE

| BILLS | AMOUNT | DATE | PAID |
|-------|--------|------|------|
|       |        |      |      |
|       |        |      |      |
|       |        |      |      |
|       |        |      |      |
|       |        |      |      |
|       |        |      |      |
|       |        |      |      |
|       |        |      |      |

## CATEGORY

| Utilities |   |   |   |   |   |
|-----------|---|---|---|---|---|
|           |   |   |   |   |   |
|           |   |   |   |   |   |
|           |   |   |   |   |   |
|           |   |   |   |   |   |
|           |   |   |   |   |   |
|           |   |   |   |   |   |
|           |   |   |   |   |   |
|           |   |   |   |   |   |

## WEEKLY

| MON | TUE | WED | THU | FRI | SAT | SUN |
|-----|-----|-----|-----|-----|-----|-----|
|     |     |     |     |     |     |     |

## CATEGORY

# EXPENDITURE

| BILLS | AMOUNT | DATE | PAID |
|-------|--------|------|------|
|       |        |      |      |
|       |        |      |      |
|       |        |      |      |
|       |        |      |      |
|       |        |      |      |
|       |        |      |      |
|       |        |      |      |
|       |        |      |      |
|       |        |      |      |
|       |        |      |      |
|       |        |      |      |
|       |        |      |      |
|       |        |      |      |
|       |        |      |      |

# CATEGORY

|  |  |  |  |  |  |
|--|--|--|--|--|--|
|  |  |  |  |  |  |
|  |  |  |  |  |  |
|  |  |  |  |  |  |
|  |  |  |  |  |  |
|  |  |  |  |  |  |
|  |  |  |  |  |  |
|  |  |  |  |  |  |
|  |  |  |  |  |  |
|  |  |  |  |  |  |
|  |  |  |  |  |  |
|  |  |  |  |  |  |
|  |  |  |  |  |  |
|  |  |  |  |  |  |
|  |  |  |  |  |  |

# CATEGORY

# SAVING PLAN

| DATE | DESCRIPTION | SAVING FOR | AMOUNT |
|------|-------------|------------|--------|
|      |             |            |        |
|      |             |            |        |
|      |             |            |        |
|      |             |            |        |
|      |             |            |        |
|      |             |            |        |
|      |             |            |        |
|      |             |            |        |
|      |             |            |        |
|      |             |            |        |
|      |             |            |        |
|      |             |            |        |
|      |             |            |        |
|      |             |            |        |
|      |             |            |        |
|      |             |            |        |
|      |             |     TOTAL: |        |

# SAVING PLAN

| DATE | DESCRIPTION | SAVING FOR | AMOUNT |
|------|-------------|------------|--------|
|      |             |            |        |
|      |             |            |        |
|      |             |            |        |
|      |             |            |        |
|      |             |            |        |
|      |             |            |        |
|      |             |            |        |
|      |             |            |        |
|      |             |            |        |
|      |             |            |        |
|      |             |            |        |
|      |             |            |        |
|      |             |            |        |
|      |             |            |        |
|      |             |            |        |
|      |             |            |        |
|      |             |   TOTAL:   |        |

| DATE | DESCRIPTION | SAVING FOR | AMOUNT |

| MONTH: | YEAR: |
|---|---|

## INCOME

| | |
|---|---|
| | |
| | |
| | |
| | |
| TOTAL: | |

## OUTCOME

| | |
|---|---|
| | |
| | |
| | |
| | |
| TOTAL: | |

## EXPENDITURE

| BILLS | AMOUNT | DATE | PAID |
|---|---|---|---|
| | | | |
| | | | |
| | | | |
| | | | |
| | | | |
| | | | |
| | | | |

## CATEGORY

| Utilities | | | | | |
|---|---|---|---|---|---|
| | | | | | |
| | | | | | |
| | | | | | |
| | | | | | |
| | | | | | |
| | | | | | |

| WEEKLY |||||||
|---|---|---|---|---|---|---|
| MON | TUE | WED | THU | FRI | SAT | SUN |
|  |  |  |  |  |  |  |

## CATEGORY

# EXPENDITURE

| BILLS | AMOUNT | DATE | PAID |
|---|---|---|---|
|  |  |  |  |
|  |  |  |  |
|  |  |  |  |
|  |  |  |  |
|  |  |  |  |
|  |  |  |  |
|  |  |  |  |
|  |  |  |  |
|  |  |  |  |
|  |  |  |  |
|  |  |  |  |
|  |  |  |  |
|  |  |  |  |
|  |  |  |  |
|  |  |  |  |

# CATEGORY

# CATEGORY

# SAVING PLAN

| DATE | DESCRIPTION | SAVING FOR | AMOUNT |
|------|-------------|------------|--------|
|      |             |            |        |
|      |             |            |        |
|      |             |            |        |
|      |             |            |        |
|      |             |            |        |
|      |             |            |        |
|      |             |            |        |
|      |             |            |        |
|      |             |            |        |
|      |             |            |        |
|      |             |            |        |
|      |             |            |        |
|      |             |            |        |
|      |             |            |        |
|      |             |            |        |
|      |             |            |        |
|      |             |            |        |
|      |             | TOTAL:     |        |

# NOTE

# NOTE